SOCIAL MEDIA MARKETING (BEGINNER-FRIENDLY)

Step-by-Step Guide to Building Your Brand and Growing Your Business Online

Gideon Richey

COPYRIGHT

Social Media Marketing (Beginner-friendly) © 2024

Gideon Richey. All rights reserved.

No part of this publication may be reproduced, distributed, or transmitted in any form or by any means, including photocopying, recording, or other electronic or mechanical methods, without the prior written permission of the author, except in the case of brief quotations embodied in critical reviews and certain other noncommercial uses permitted by copyright law.

CONTENTS

INTRODUCTION..6
    Purpose of This Book........................10
CHAPTER 1..**12**
    The Basics of Social Media Marketing..12
        What is Social Media Marketing?......13
        How It Differs From Traditional Marketing.. 14
        The Benefits of Social Media for Small Businesses...15
        Popular Social Media Platforms for Small Businesses.............................17
        Which Platform is Right for Your Business?..21
CHAPTER 2..**24**
    Setting Up Your Social Media Profiles..24
        Creating a Professional Business Profile..24
        Importance of a Strong Bio, Profile Picture, and Cover Image................. 29
        Consistency Across Platforms......... 31
            Examples of Businesses That Do This Well..33
CHAPTER 3..**36**

Developing a Social Media Strategy.....36
  Why You Need a Social Media Strategy..................................36
  Creating a Content Calendar........... 41
  Measuring Success with Analytics... 44

CHAPTER 4..48
Content Creation for Beginners........... 48
  Types of Content That Work........... 48
  Which Content Works Best on Different Platforms?......................... 52
  How to Create Engaging Posts........ 53
  Free and Affordable Tools for Creating Social Media Content....................... 56

CHAPTER 5.. 60
Growing Your Audience Organically..... 60
  What is Organic Growth?.................. 61
  How to Grow Your Followers Without Paying for Ads................................... 62
  Building Relationships with Your Audience.. 64
  Collaborating with Influencers and Other Businesses............................. 66

CHAPTER 6.. 70
Using Paid Advertising on Social Media...

3

70
    The Basics of Facebook and Instagram Ads...................................72
    Budgeting for Social Media Ads.......77

CHAPTER 7..**80**
  Managing Your Time and Resources....80
    Social Media Management Tools.....81
    Outsourcing Social Media Management.....................................85
      When and How to Hire Freelancers or Agencies to Help with Your Social Media................................85

CHAPTER 8..**92**
  Overcoming Common Challenges........92
    What to Do When You Don't See Results Right Away............................92
    Handling Negative Comments and Reviews..97

CONCLUSION.. **102**
    Next Steps for Your Social Media Success..104

Don't wait for the perfect moment to begin. Start now, wherever you are. Every small step you take on social media brings you closer to your goals. Consistency is key. Keep showing up, and the results will follow.

INTRODUCTION

In today's digital world, social media has become a vital tool for businesses of all sizes. It's hard to imagine marketing without it. **But why exactly is social media so important for small businesses?** The answer lies in its ability to level the playing field. Gone are the days when only big brands with huge budgets could dominate the market. Now, even a small business can create a strong presence and compete with the giants—all thanks to social media.

Social media has completely changed the way businesses interact with their customers. Before, marketing was largely a one-way street. Companies would push out advertisements on TV, radio, or in print, hoping to catch the attention of potential customers. There was little room for interaction, and feedback was slow.

Social media changed all of that. Now, businesses can engage directly with their audience in real-time. It allows brands to not only share their message but also to listen to what customers are saying, respond to their concerns, and build relationships. This shift has made marketing more personal, dynamic, and interactive. It has transformed marketing from just "talking at" customers to having conversations with them.

Moreover, social media allows businesses to target their marketing efforts more precisely. Whether it's through paid ads or organic content, you can tailor your message to reach the people who are most likely to be interested in your products or services. This is a game-changer for small businesses with limited budgets, as it means your efforts can be focused and effective.

One of the most exciting things about social media is that it gives small businesses the opportunity to compete with bigger, more established brands. With traditional advertising, larger companies often have the upper hand because they can afford expensive ad campaigns on TV, billboards, or magazines. Small businesses, on the other hand, had fewer options to reach a large audience.

But with social media, the playing field is more level. It doesn't cost anything to create a profile on platforms like Facebook, Instagram, or Twitter. With the right strategy, even a small business with a limited budget can build a loyal following, grow its brand, and reach potential customers worldwide.

Social media also allows for creativity to shine. A small business that knows how to engage with its audience in fun, interesting, or helpful ways can quickly build a community of dedicated followers. Authenticity and connection often matter more to today's consumers than a flashy ad, and this is where small businesses can truly thrive. Whether it's through storytelling, behind-the-scenes looks, or offering valuable content, a small business can stand out and connect with people in a way that bigger brands often struggle to do.

Purpose of This Book

This book is designed to guide you, the small business owner, through the world of social media marketing. If you're new to social media or feel overwhelmed by the sheer number of platforms and strategies, don't worry—you're not alone. The goal of this book is to break everything down into simple, easy-to-follow steps that anyone can understand and implement.

I'll cover the basics of setting up your social media profiles, how to create content that engages your audience, and how to grow your following without needing to spend a fortune. You'll also learn how to develop a strategy that works for your business and how to track your success using simple tools. Whether you're a complete beginner or you've dabbled in social media but want to improve, this book will give you the knowledge and confidence to succeed.

The key takeaway? Social media marketing isn't just for big brands with big budgets. It's for any business willing to put in the time and effort to connect with their audience. With the right approach, even the smallest businesses can make a big impact. So, let's get started and help your small business shine on social media!

CHAPTER 1

The Basics of Social Media Marketing

Social media marketing is one of the most powerful tools available to small businesses today. It's a way to connect with your customers, build your brand, and drive sales—all without needing a huge budget. In this chapter, I'll break down what social media marketing is, how it differs from traditional marketing, and why it's so beneficial for small businesses. I'll also explore the most popular social media platforms and help you figure out which one is right for your business.

What is Social Media Marketing?

At its core, social media marketing is the use of social media platforms—like Facebook, Instagram, Twitter, LinkedIn, and others—to promote your business. It involves creating and sharing content (such as posts, photos, videos, and ads) to engage with your audience, attract new customers, and boost your business.

Unlike traditional advertising, which focuses on one-way communication (where a business sends a message to potential customers), social media marketing allows for two-way interaction. You're not just telling people about your products—you're having conversations, building relationships, and listening to what your audience has to say. This makes social media a more personal and interactive form of marketing.

How It Differs From Traditional Marketing

Traditional marketing includes things like print ads, billboards, TV commercials, and radio spots. These methods are usually expensive and target a broad audience, hoping to capture the attention of potential customers. Once the ad is out there, the business has little control over who sees it or how people respond.

Social media marketing, on the other hand, allows you to target a specific audience—people who are most likely to be interested in your product or service. You can also engage directly with your followers, responding to their comments, answering questions, and building a loyal community around your brand. Social media is often more cost-effective than traditional advertising, especially for small businesses with limited budgets. Best of all, you can track your results in real time and adjust your strategy as needed to maximize your efforts.

The Benefits of Social Media for Small Businesses

Now, let's look at why social media is such a powerful tool for small businesses:

1. **Reach a Wider Audience:** Social media platforms have billions of active users. By establishing a presence on social media, your business can reach a global audience that you wouldn't be able to access through

traditional marketing alone. Even if you're focused on serving a local market, social media can help you reach more people in your community who may not have heard of your business otherwise.

2. **Build a Loyal Customer Base:** Social media allows you to interact with your customers directly. When you consistently engage with your audience—responding to comments, sharing valuable content, and showing the human side of your brand—you can build strong, lasting relationships. These relationships often lead to customer loyalty, as people are more likely to support businesses they feel connected to.

3. **Increase Brand Visibility:** One of the greatest benefits of social media is that it helps increase your brand's visibility. By regularly posting content and engaging with your followers, you can keep your business top of mind. When someone in your audience needs a product or service that you offer, they'll be more likely to think of you. Plus, as people share your content with their own networks, your reach expands even further, increasing your brand's exposure to new potential customers.

Popular Social Media Platforms for Small Businesses

Each social media platform has its own unique features and audience. It's important to choose the platform that best fits your business and marketing goals. Let's take a closer look at some of the most popular platforms for small businesses:

1. **Facebook:** Facebook is one of the largest social media platforms in the world, with over 2.8 billion active users. It's great for small businesses because it offers a wide range of tools to help you reach your audience, including business pages, paid advertising, and the ability to join groups relevant to your industry. If your business serves a broad audience, Facebook is a good platform to start with.

2. **Instagram:** Instagram is a visual platform focused on sharing photos and videos. It's especially popular with younger audiences

and is a great choice for businesses that rely on visual content, such as fashion, food, or fitness brands. Instagram offers features like Stories, IGTV, and Reels, which allow you to create engaging content and showcase your products in creative ways.

3. **Twitter:** Twitter is a platform where users share short, text-based messages called tweets. It's ideal for businesses that want to share news, updates, and interact quickly with their audience. Twitter is great for real-time engagement, making it a good platform for businesses that want to stay connected with trends or provide customer support.

4. **LinkedIn:** LinkedIn is a professional networking platform that's perfect for B2B (business-to-business) companies or businesses that want to connect with other professionals. It's a great platform for sharing industry insights, networking, and establishing your business as a thought leader in your field.

5. **Pinterest:** Pinterest is a visual discovery platform where users search for ideas and inspiration. It's especially useful for businesses in industries like home décor, fashion, food, and DIY. If your business has a lot of visual content that can inspire or educate, Pinterest can be a powerful tool for driving traffic to your website.

6. **TikTok:** TikTok is a fast-growing platform focused on short-form videos. It's popular with a younger audience and allows businesses to showcase their products and services in fun, creative ways. If your business is targeting Gen Z or millennial customers, TikTok is worth exploring.

Which Platform is Right for Your Business?

The best platform for your business depends on several factors, including your target audience, the type of content you plan to share, and your overall goals. If you're just starting out, it's usually a good idea to focus on one or two platforms that align with your audience and business type. **For example:**

- If you run a visually-driven business like a bakery, restaurant, or clothing boutique, Instagram and Pinterest may be your best bet.
- If you're a local service provider (like a real estate agent or fitness coach), Facebook might be the most effective way to reach potential customers in your area.
- For a business that sells to other businesses, LinkedIn can help you connect with professionals and decision-makers in your industry.

As you grow more comfortable with social media marketing, you can expand to other platforms and experiment with different types of content.

In summary, social media marketing offers small businesses an affordable and effective way to connect with customers, increase brand visibility, and grow their audience. By choosing the right platforms and focusing on building genuine relationships with your audience, you can take full advantage of the benefits social media has to offer.

CHAPTER 2

Setting Up Your Social Media Profiles

Before you dive into social media marketing, it's important to ensure that your business looks professional online. This chapter will guide you through setting up professional social media profiles that reflect your brand and attract the right audience. I'll cover how to create a strong profile on key platforms, the importance of having a cohesive brand across all platforms, and why consistency matters.

Creating a Professional Business Profile

Your social media profile is the first impression people will get of your business, so it's essential to make it count. Here's a step-by-step guide to help you set up professional profiles on the most popular platforms:

Step 1: Choose the Right Platforms Start by deciding which social media platforms make the most sense for your business. As discussed in Chapter 1, Facebook, Instagram, Twitter, LinkedIn, and others all offer unique features. Choose the platforms where your target audience is most active.

Step 2: Sign Up for a Business Account Many social media platforms offer different account types, including personal and business accounts. Always sign up for a business account (or convert your existing one to a business profile) to access extra features like insights, analytics, and advertising tools. Here's a brief guide for setting up business accounts on key platforms:

- **Facebook:** Go to Facebook for Business and create a page for your business.
- **Instagram:** Sign up for an Instagram account, then go to your settings and switch to a professional account.
- **Twitter:** You can use a regular Twitter account for business, but make sure you specify that it's for your company and fill in all the details.
- **LinkedIn:** Set up a LinkedIn Company Page to showcase your business and connect with professionals.

Step 3: Fill in Your Profile Information

Once your business account is set up, it's time to fill in the details. Here's what you need to focus on:

1. **Profile Picture:** Use a high-quality image of your logo or a recognizable symbol that represents your business. Make sure it's clear, professional, and consistent across all platforms. Your profile picture should instantly tell people who you are.

2. **Cover Image (if applicable):** Some platforms, like Facebook and LinkedIn, allow you to upload a larger cover image. Use this space to showcase something visually appealing about your business, such as your product, a key message, or even a slogan.

Make sure the cover image complements your profile picture and brand colors.

3. **Bio or About Section:** Your bio is where you introduce your business. Keep it short, clear, and engaging. Highlight what makes your business unique, what you offer, and why people should follow you. Include keywords that are relevant to your industry to help people find you easily. Don't forget to add a link to your website or online store.

    Here's a quick formula for a great business bio:
    - **Who you are** (your business name)
    - **What you do** (products or services)
    - **Why it matters** (what makes you unique or valuable)

- **Call to action** (invite people to visit your website, contact you, or shop)

4. **Example for a local bakery:** "Sweet Treats Bakery 🏠 | Freshly baked goods daily | Custom cakes for every occasion | Visit us at SweetTreatsBakery.com to order your next treat!"

Step 4: Contact Information Always provide contact details. Whether it's an email address, phone number, or location (if you have a physical store), make it easy for people to get in touch with you.

Importance of a Strong Bio, Profile Picture, and Cover Image

Your profile picture, bio, and cover image are crucial because they create your business's first impression on potential followers. Here's why these elements matter:

- **Profile Picture:** This is the face of your business online. It needs to be professional and recognizable so that people can identify your brand quickly, even if they just see your profile in a list of search results or on someone else's feed.
- **Bio:** A strong bio tells people what you're about in just a few seconds. It's the quickest way to communicate your value to a potential customer. A weak or confusing bio can make people lose interest or misunderstand what you offer.
- **Cover Image:** The cover image is a great way to reinforce your brand and showcase

your personality. It should be eye-catching but not overly complicated. Keep it aligned with your brand's visual identity and message.

Consistency Across Platforms

Consistency is key when it comes to building a strong online presence. Your brand should feel cohesive across all social media platforms, from your profile picture and bio to your tone of voice and posting style. When people see your brand on different platforms, they should instantly recognize it.

Here's how to maintain consistency:

1. **Visual Branding:** Use the same logo, profile picture, and color scheme across all your

platforms. This creates a unified look that helps people recognize your business no matter where they see it. For example, if your logo is blue and white, make sure your cover images, posts, and any visuals you use also incorporate those colors.

2. **Tone of Voice:** Whether your brand is casual, professional, or playful, keep the tone of your posts consistent across platforms. If you're lighthearted on Instagram, don't be overly formal on LinkedIn. Find a tone that fits your brand and stick with it.

3. **Posting Style:** While each platform has its own features (Instagram focuses on images, Twitter on text, etc.), your overall content

style should remain consistent. For example, if you use humor or storytelling in your Instagram posts, try to incorporate the same elements into your Facebook and Twitter content.

Examples of Businesses That Do This Well

- **Nike:** Nike is known for its strong, consistent branding across all platforms. Whether you see their logo, their famous tagline "Just Do It," or the empowering tone of their posts, you always know it's Nike. They use the same profile picture, a consistent tone, and visuals that reflect their brand's values of inspiration and athleticism.
- **Glossier:** This beauty brand has mastered consistency across platforms. Their

minimalist pink-and-white color scheme, youthful tone of voice, and product-focused visuals are instantly recognizable, whether you're on their Instagram or visiting their website. Glossier creates a unified brand experience for their followers, no matter where they interact with the brand.

By maintaining consistency across platforms, your business can create a strong, recognizable brand presence. This helps build trust with your audience and ensures that people know exactly who you are and what you offer, no matter where they see your content.

Social media isn't just about numbers—it's about building real connections. Each follower, like, and comment is a person who is interested in your business. Treat them with care, and you'll create a loyal community that supports your growth.

CHAPTER 3

Developing a Social Media Strategy

A strong social media presence doesn't happen by accident. To succeed in social media marketing, you need a well-thought-out plan that helps you stay focused and organized. This chapter will walk you through why developing a social media strategy is essential, how to set goals, and the importance of knowing your audience. I'll also cover how to plan your content in advance and track your progress using analytics.

Why You Need a Social Media Strategy

Without a strategy, your social media efforts can feel random and unproductive. A social media strategy helps you define what you want to achieve and how you'll get there. It's like a roadmap that guides your actions, ensuring that every post, comment, and interaction works toward a larger goal.

Here are three key reasons why having a strategy is crucial for small businesses:

1. **Setting Clear Goals** Before you start posting, you need to know *why* you're doing it. What do you hope to achieve with your social media efforts? Here are some common goals:

    - **Brand Awareness:** If you're just starting out or want more people to know about your business, you'll focus on increasing visibility and getting your name out there. This means posting regularly and making sure your content reaches new potential customers.

- **Customer Engagement:** Want to build a community around your brand? Social media is a great tool for interacting with your audience, answering their questions, and encouraging them to engage with your posts through likes, comments, and shares.
- **Driving Sales:** If your goal is to increase sales, your strategy should focus on promoting products, offering

special deals, and leading followers to your website or online store.

2. Clear goals give you something to measure your progress against. Without goals, it's difficult to know if your social media efforts are working.

3. **Identifying Your Target Audience** Knowing *who* you're talking to is just as important as knowing what you want to say. Your target audience is the group of people most likely to be interested in your products or services. Understanding your audience helps you create content that speaks directly to them and meets their needs.

To identify your target audience, consider factors like:

- **Demographics:** What is their age, gender, location, or income level?
- **Interests:** What are their hobbies or passions? What kind of content do they enjoy online?
- **Challenges:** What problems or challenges do they face that your business can help solve?

4. Once you know your audience, you can tailor your content to them. For example, a small bakery might target local customers who are looking for delicious treats, while a tech startup might focus on young professionals interested in the latest gadgets.

5. **Creating a Content Calendar** Consistency is key when it comes to social media

marketing, and the best way to stay consistent is by planning your content ahead of time. This is where a content calendar comes in handy.

Creating a Content Calendar

A content calendar is simply a plan that outlines what you're going to post and when. By organizing your posts in advance, you can avoid last-minute stress and make sure you're posting regularly.

Benefits of Using a Content Calendar:

- **Staying Consistent:** Posting consistently is important for staying on your followers' radar. If you post every day for a week and then disappear for a month, people might forget about your business. A content calendar helps you keep a regular schedule, so you're always in front of your audience.

- **Saving Time:** Planning your content ahead saves you time in the long run. Instead of scrambling to come up with ideas on the spot, you'll have everything laid out in advance. This gives you more time to focus on running your business.

- **Keeping Content Balanced:** A calendar helps you ensure that you're posting a variety of content. For example, you can schedule product promotions, customer testimonials, helpful tips, and behind-the-scenes posts to keep things interesting.

How to Create a Content Calendar:

1. **Decide on Your Posting Frequency:** How often do you want to post? This could be daily, a few times a week, or weekly. Choose a schedule that's realistic for you.

2. **Choose Your Content Types:** Think about the different types of content that will interest your audience. This could include blog posts, product photos, videos, infographics, or even live streams.

3. **Plan in Advance:** Use a simple calendar (Google Calendar, Excel, or even a physical planner) to map out your posts for the week or month. For each post, write down the topic, the platform you'll post it on, and the time you plan to post.

Measuring Success with Analytics

Once you've started posting consistently, how do you know if your social media strategy is working? This is where analytics come into play. Social media platforms offer free tools that let you track how well your content is performing.

Key Social Media Metrics:

1. **Engagement:** Engagement includes likes, comments, shares, and retweets. It shows how much people are interacting with your content. High engagement means that your posts are resonating with your audience.
2. **Reach:** Reach is the number of people who see your content. The more people who see

your posts, the more potential customers you're reaching.

3. **Followers:** Your follower count is the number of people who have chosen to see your posts in their feed. Growing your followers means that more people are interested in your business.

By regularly reviewing these metrics, you can see which types of content are working and which ones aren't. For example, if you notice that your product photos get more engagement than your text posts, you can focus on posting more images.

Free Tools for Tracking Analytics:

- **Facebook Insights:** If you have a Facebook business page, you can use Insights to track how your posts are performing, see which ones get the most engagement, and learn more about your audience.

- **Instagram Insights:** Available for business accounts, Instagram Insights gives you data on post engagement, reach, and follower growth. You can also see when your followers are most active, which helps you post at the best times.

- **Twitter Analytics:** Twitter offers a free analytics dashboard where you can view tweet performance, follower growth, and more.

- **Google Analytics:** If you're using social media to drive traffic to your website, Google Analytics lets you track how much of that traffic is coming from your social media platforms.

In conclusion, having a social media strategy is essential for any small business looking to succeed in the digital world. By setting clear goals, identifying your target audience, planning your content in advance, and regularly measuring your progress, you can ensure that your social media efforts are effective and aligned with your business goals.

CHAPTER 4

Content Creation for Beginners

Creating content for social media can feel overwhelming, especially when you're just starting out. But don't worry—you don't need to be a professional designer or writer to create posts that grab attention. In this chapter, I'll explore the types of content that work well on social media, offer tips for creating engaging posts, and recommend free and affordable tools that make content creation easier.

Types of Content That Work

Social media is all about visuals and stories. People are drawn to posts that catch their eye and make them want to engage. Depending on the platform, certain types of content perform better than others. Here are some popular content types and where they shine:

1. **Images**
    - **Why they work:** People process images faster than text. A well-designed image can quickly communicate your message and create a lasting impression.
    - **Best platforms:** Instagram, Facebook, Pinterest.
    - **Examples:** High-quality photos of your products, behind-the-scenes shots, or user-generated content like customer photos.

2. **Videos**
    - **Why they work:** Videos are highly engaging and can convey more information than a static image. They're perfect for showing how your product works or sharing testimonials.
    - **Best platforms:** Instagram, Facebook, YouTube, TikTok.
    - **Examples:** Product demos, tutorials, customer reviews, or company updates.

3. **Stories**
    - **Why they work:** Stories are temporary posts that last 24 hours. They're a great way to share quick

updates, promotions, or personal content that doesn't need to be permanent.

- **Best platforms:** Instagram, Facebook, Snapchat.
- **Examples:** Limited-time offers, new arrivals, or "behind the scenes" content that shows your business in action.

4. **Live Streams**

    - **Why they work:** Live streaming allows you to interact with your audience in real-time, creating a sense of connection and urgency.
    - **Best platforms:** Instagram Live, Facebook Live, YouTube Live.

- o **Examples:** Q&A sessions, product launches, live tutorials, or customer interaction events.

Which Content Works Best on Different Platforms?

Not all platforms are the same, and neither is the type of content that works best on each one. Here's a quick breakdown of what works well on popular social media platforms:

- **Instagram:** High-quality photos, short videos, and stories. This platform is all about visuals.
- **Facebook:** A mix of photos, videos, and text posts. Facebook is great for both images and longer written content.

- **Twitter:** Short, snappy text posts with images or videos. Twitter is fast-paced, so quick, engaging updates work best.
- **LinkedIn:** Professional articles, business updates, and industry news. LinkedIn is more about thought leadership and connecting with a professional audience.
- **YouTube:** Long-form video content like tutorials, how-tos, and product reviews. This is the go-to platform for video content.

How to Create Engaging Posts

Creating content is one thing, but getting people to engage with it is another. Here are some tips to make your posts more engaging and encourage your audience to interact:

1. **Write Captions That Get Attention** Your caption is what draws people into your post. It's your chance to add context, ask questions, or tell a story. Here are some tips for writing better captions:
    - **Keep it short and sweet:** Social media users often scroll quickly, so make your point early in the caption.
    - **Ask questions:** Engaging your audience directly encourages them to leave comments. **For example,** "What's your favorite product from our new collection?"
    - **Use a call to action:** Encourage your followers to take action by saying

things like "Shop now," "Tag a friend," or "Check the link in our bio."

2. **Use Hashtags and Tagging for More Visibility** Hashtags and tagging are simple ways to boost your content's reach. Hashtags help people discover your posts, while tagging other accounts or locations can increase engagement.

    - **Hashtags:** Use relevant hashtags that relate to your industry or audience. **For example**, if you run a small bakery, hashtags like #homemadebaking or #smallbusinesslove can help new people find your content.

- **Tagging:** Tag relevant accounts in your posts, such as customers or partner businesses. You can also tag your location to make your post discoverable to people nearby.

Free and Affordable Tools for Creating Social Media Content

You don't need expensive software to create high-quality social media content. There are plenty of beginner-friendly tools that can help you design professional-looking posts without breaking the bank. Here are a few of the best tools:

1. **Canva**
    - **What it is:** Canva is a simple, drag-and-drop design tool that's perfect for creating social media

posts, flyers, business cards, and more. It has a wide range of free templates that are easy to customize, even if you're not a designer.

- **Why it's great:** Canva offers a free version with plenty of design features and pre-made templates for different platforms (e.g., Instagram posts, Facebook covers). Plus, it has a library of free images, icons, and fonts.

2. **Adobe Spark**

    - **What it is:** Adobe Spark is another easy-to-use design tool that allows you to create graphics, videos, and web pages. It's designed for beginners and offers simple templates for social media content.

- **Why it's great:** Adobe Spark has both free and paid versions, and it's ideal for creating visually appealing posts quickly. It also offers some video creation features, making it versatile.

3. **Unsplash**
    - **What it is:** Unsplash is a website that offers a huge collection of high-quality, free stock images. You can use these images in your posts, even for commercial purposes.
    - **Why it's great:** If you don't have access to professional photos or don't

have time to take your own, Unsplash offers stunning, free images that can help make your posts stand out.

4. **Pexels**

    - **What it is:** Pexels is similar to Unsplash, offering free stock images and videos that you can use for your social media content.

    - **Why it's great:** In addition to photos, Pexels offers free videos, which are perfect for creating engaging posts on platforms like Instagram and Facebook.

By using these tools and strategies, creating engaging social media content becomes much more manageable, even for beginners.

CHAPTER 5

Growing Your Audience Organically

One of the most important parts of social media marketing is building a genuine connection with your audience. While paid ads can speed up growth, organic growth—gaining followers naturally without paying—is often more sustainable in the long run. In this chapter, I'll explore what organic growth is, how to grow your followers, and strategies for engaging with your audience. I'll also talk about how collaborating with influencers and other businesses can help boost your presence.

What is Organic Growth?

Organic growth on social media means increasing your followers, likes, and engagement without spending money on ads. It happens when people discover your content, like it, and decide to follow you. They may find you through hashtags, recommendations, or by sharing your posts with their friends.

Organic growth takes time, but it's valuable because it builds a loyal, engaged audience. These are people who genuinely like what you do and are more likely to become customers. Organic growth relies on the quality of your content, your interactions with followers, and how well you understand your audience.

How to Grow Your Followers Without Paying for Ads

Here are some simple yet effective ways to grow your social media followers organically:

1. **Post Consistently** One of the most important ways to attract new followers is to stay active. Posting regularly shows that your business is engaged and provides fresh content for your followers to enjoy. Use a content calendar to plan posts ahead and maintain consistency.

2. **Use Relevant Hashtags** Hashtags help people discover your posts. By using popular and relevant hashtags, you can get your content in front of a wider audience. For example, if you own a bakery, hashtags like

#bakinglove or #homemadegoodies could help food lovers find your page.

3. **Engage with Other Accounts** Follow and interact with other accounts in your niche. Leave thoughtful comments, like their posts, and share content when appropriate. This will help you get noticed by their followers, who may decide to follow you in return.

4. **Post User-Generated Content** Encourage your customers to share their experiences with your product or service on social media. When they tag you in their posts, share it on your page (with their permission). This not only creates authentic content but also builds a sense of community.

5. **Optimize Your Profile** Make sure your profile is fully optimized with a clear bio, profile picture, and contact information. A well-designed profile makes it easier for potential followers to understand what your business is about and why they should follow you.

Building Relationships with Your Audience

Growing your followers is important, but building strong relationships with them is even more critical. When you engage with your audience, you're more likely to turn casual followers into loyal fans. Here's how to do it:

1. **Engage with Comments, Likes, and Messages** Responding to comments, likes,

and direct messages is a simple yet effective way to show that you care about your audience. Acknowledge their feedback, answer their questions, and thank them for their support. This helps create a two-way conversation and makes followers feel valued.

2. **Host Giveaways** Giveaways are a great way to generate excitement and attract new followers. Offer one of your products or services as a prize and encourage participants to follow your page, like the post, and tag a friend. This not only increases engagement but also helps you reach new potential customers.

3. **Use Polls and Q&A Sessions** Polls and Q&A sessions are interactive features that can boost engagement. Ask your followers for their opinions on new products, services, or ideas. You can also host Q&A sessions where you answer questions about your business, industry, or products. This keeps followers involved and makes them feel like part of the conversation.

Collaborating with Influencers and Other Businesses

Collaborations are a powerful way to reach new audiences. Partnering with influencers or other businesses that share your values and target audience can help you grow faster and gain credibility.

1. **Finding Micro-Influencers in Your Niche** Micro-influencers are social media users with a smaller, but highly engaged following. They are often more affordable to work with than larger influencers and can help you reach a specific audience. To find micro-influencers, look for people who are active in your industry or who already support similar brands. Reach out to them to discuss potential collaborations, such as promoting your products or featuring them in their posts.

2. **Partnering with Other Local Businesses for Cross-Promotion** Another great way to grow your audience is by teaming up with other businesses, especially if they

complement what you do. For example, if you own a coffee shop, you could partner with a local bakery. You can promote each other's products on social media and even offer joint giveaways or discounts. This exposes your business to a new audience that may be interested in what you offer.

Growing your social media following organically takes time and effort, but the results are worth it. By focusing on building strong relationships with your audience and collaborating with others in your industry, you can create a loyal community that supports your business and spreads the word about your brand.

No one is an expert on day one. Whether you're learning how to create content, engage with your audience, or run ads, remember that every challenge is an opportunity to grow. Keep pushing yourself, and the skills will come with time.

Great things come from small beginnings. Whether you have ten followers or ten thousand, keep your vision in mind. Every post you create and every person you connect with is part of building something bigger.

CHAPTER 6

Using Paid Advertising on Social Media

While growing your social media audience organically is essential, adding paid advertising to your strategy can help you reach more people, faster. Social media ads allow you to target specific audiences, promote your products or services, and boost your brand's visibility. This chapter covers how paid ads work on social media, with a focus on platforms like Facebook and Instagram. It also looks at budgeting and tracking performance to ensure you get the most out of your investment.

What are social media ads?

Social media ads are paid advertisements that appear on platforms like Facebook, Instagram, Twitter, and LinkedIn. These ads can take various forms, including image posts, videos, and carousel ads (multiple images or videos in a single post). Businesses pay to have these ads shown to specific audiences, allowing them to promote their products, services, or brand directly to people who are most likely to be interested.

Why should small businesses use social media ads?

For small businesses, social media ads can be a powerful tool. Unlike traditional ads (like billboards or TV commercials), social media ads are affordable and highly targeted. You can choose who sees your ads based on factors like age, location, interests, and even past behavior online. This means your message reaches people who are more likely to become customers.

Paid ads also provide immediate results. While organic growth takes time, paid ads can drive traffic to your website or increase your social media following in just a few days. Whether you want to raise brand awareness, promote a sale, or launch a new product, social media ads help you get noticed by the right audience.

The Basics of Facebook and Instagram Ads

Facebook and Instagram are two of the most popular platforms for social media advertising. Both platforms are owned by Meta, which means their ad tools and options are very similar. Let's look at how to create a basic ad campaign on these platforms.

How to create a simple ad campaign:

1. **Choose Your Objective**

    Before creating an ad, decide what you want to achieve. Do you want to drive more people to your website? Increase your page's followers? Or get more people to engage with your posts? Facebook and Instagram offer different campaign objectives like "Traffic," "Engagement," and "Conversions." Pick the one that best fits your goal.

2. **Set Your Audience**

   One of the biggest advantages of social media ads is audience targeting. You can target your ideal customers based on age, location, gender, and interests. For example, if you run a small fitness business, you might target people in your city who are interested in health, wellness, and exercise.

3. **Design Your Ad**

   You don't need to be a professional designer to create a good-looking ad. You can use free tools like Canva to design simple yet attractive images or videos for your ad. Make sure your ad includes a clear call to action (CTA), like "Shop Now," "Learn More," or "Sign Up Today."

4. **Set Your Budget**

   Decide how much money you want to spend on your ad. Facebook and Instagram allow you to set a daily or total budget for your campaign. A daily budget means your ad will spend a certain amount each day, while a total budget sets a limit for the entire campaign. You can start small, even with just $5 a day, and see how your ad performs.

Understanding Ad Targeting

Ad targeting is the key to reaching the right people with your message. Facebook and Instagram allow you to get specific with your targeting by using different factors:

- **Demographics**: Target people based on their age, gender, education, or relationship status.
- **Location**: Show your ads to people in specific cities, states, or countries.
- **Interests**: Reach people based on their hobbies, interests, or behaviors (e.g., people who like fitness or cooking).
- **Custom Audiences**: You can also create custom audiences using data like your email list or website visitors.

By fine-tuning your audience settings, you can ensure your ads are seen by people who are most likely to be interested in what you offer, improving your ad's performance and saving you money.

Budgeting for Social Media Ads

How much should you spend?

When it comes to budgeting for social media ads, the amount you spend depends on your business goals and how fast you want to see results. A good rule of thumb for beginners is to start small and increase your budget as you see what works. For example, you could begin with $5 or $10 per day for a week or two, then adjust your spending based on the ad's performance.

If you're running a campaign for a specific event, product launch, or sale, you might want to set a total budget instead of a daily one. This allows you to spend more over a short period to get faster results.

Tracking Ad Performance to Get the Best ROI

Once your ad is running, it's essential to track how it's performing. Social media platforms provide detailed analytics to help you measure success. Here are some key metrics to watch:

- **Impressions**: The number of times your ad was shown.
- **Reach**: The number of unique users who saw your ad.
- **Engagement**: How many people interacted with your ad (likes, shares, comments).
- **Click-Through Rate (CTR)**: The percentage of people who clicked on your ad after seeing it.

- **Conversions**: The number of people who completed a desired action, like signing up for a newsletter or making a purchase.

By reviewing these metrics, you can determine whether your ad is working. If you notice that your ad isn't performing as expected, you can make adjustments to improve its effectiveness. For example, you could try changing the audience, tweaking the ad design, or adjusting your CTA.

Paid advertising on social media is a valuable way to boost your brand and reach a wider audience. By setting clear goals, targeting the right people, and carefully managing your budget, you can create successful campaigns that help your business grow.

CHAPTER 7

Managing Your Time and Resources

Managing social media for your small business can be time-consuming. Between creating content, engaging with followers, and analyzing performance, it may start to feel overwhelming, especially if you're doing it all on your own. But with the right tools and strategies, you can streamline your social media efforts and make the process much more efficient. This chapter explores how to save time by using social media management tools and outsourcing tasks when necessary.

Social Media Management Tools

Managing multiple social media accounts can be challenging, but social media management tools are designed to make it easier. These tools help you plan, schedule, and monitor your content across different platforms from one dashboard. Let's take a closer look at some popular options.

Introduction to Tools Like Hootsuite, Buffer, and Later

1. **Hootsuite**:

    Hootsuite is one of the most popular social media management tools. It allows you to manage multiple platforms like Facebook, Instagram, Twitter, and LinkedIn all in one place. You can schedule posts, track engagement, and even respond to messages directly through the tool. Hootsuite also provides analytics to help you measure the performance of your posts.

2. **Buffer**:

   Buffer is a simpler tool, ideal for small businesses just starting out. It lets you schedule posts across different social media platforms and offers an easy-to-use interface. You can plan content ahead of time and review how your posts are performing through basic analytics.

3. **Later**:

   Later is especially useful for Instagram, although it supports other platforms as well. It features a visual content calendar that allows you to drag and drop posts into your schedule, making it easy to plan your Instagram grid. Later also offers tools for analyzing the best times to post and tracking engagement.

How to Use Scheduling Tools to Save Time

Scheduling tools can significantly reduce the amount of time you spend on social media management. Instead of manually posting content each day, you can schedule posts in advance and let the tool handle the rest. Here's how to make the most of these tools:

- **Batch Your Content Creation**: Set aside a specific time each week or month to create all your social media content. Once you have a batch of posts ready, you can upload them to a scheduling tool and plan out your content calendar in one sitting.

- **Stay Consistent**:

Posting consistently is key to growing your audience, and scheduling tools help you stick to a regular posting schedule. You can decide in advance how often you want to post and use the tool to ensure you never miss a day.

- **Analyze and Adjust**:

After scheduling your posts, make sure to review the performance data these tools provide. Check which posts are getting the most engagement and adjust your strategy accordingly. For example, if certain times of day or types of content perform better, you can focus on those moving forward.

Outsourcing Social Media Management

As your business grows, you may find it harder to manage all your social media activities on your own. This is where outsourcing can come in handy. Whether you hire a freelancer or an agency, outsourcing can help you maintain a strong social media presence without stretching yourself too thin.

When and How to Hire Freelancers or Agencies to Help with Your Social Media

When should you outsource?

You might consider outsourcing social media management when:

- You don't have enough time to manage your social media accounts effectively.
- You're struggling to stay consistent with posting or engaging with followers.
- You want to focus more on other aspects of your business, such as product development or customer service.
- You feel your social media skills aren't strong enough to achieve your goals, and you need professional help to take your strategy to the next level.

Hiring a Freelancer

Freelancers can be a great option for small businesses with a limited budget. You can find social media managers on platforms like Upwork or Fiverr who specialize in content creation, strategy, or community management. When hiring a freelancer, here's what to consider:

- **Check Their Experience**: Make sure they have experience managing social media accounts for businesses like yours. Ask for examples of their previous work and results they've achieved.
- **Clarify Responsibilities**: Clearly define what tasks you need help with—whether it's creating content, scheduling posts, or responding to messages. Setting expectations upfront will help you avoid confusion later.
- **Agree on Payment Terms**: Freelancers usually charge by the hour or by the project. Discuss and agree on payment terms before

starting the work to avoid any misunderstandings.

Hiring an Agency

If your business is ready to invest in a more comprehensive social media strategy, you might consider hiring a social media marketing agency. Agencies typically offer a range of services, including content creation, strategy development, and paid advertising management. While agencies can be more expensive than freelancers, they often bring more experience and a team of specialists who can help your business grow faster.

Here's what to keep in mind when choosing an agency:

- **Look for Niche Experience**: Find an agency that has experience working with businesses in your industry. They'll have a better understanding of your target audience and what type of content resonates with them.
- **Ask for Case Studies**: Reputable agencies will be able to show you case studies or success stories from their previous clients. This can give you a sense of how they've helped other businesses achieve their social media goals.
- **Evaluate Their Communication**: Good communication is key to a successful partnership. Make sure the agency is

responsive and willing to keep you updated on their progress regularly.

Managing social media can feel like a full-time job, but with the right tools and resources, you can streamline the process and make it much more manageable. Whether you use social media management tools to schedule posts or outsource the work to a professional, the goal is to free up your time so you can focus on what matters most—growing your business.

You don't have to get everything right the first time. The important thing is that you're making progress. Each post, each interaction, and each new follower is a step toward success. Keep improving and trust the process.

CHAPTER 8

Overcoming Common Challenges

Social media marketing is a powerful tool for small businesses, but it's not without its challenges. When you first start, it can be frustrating if you don't see immediate results or have to deal with negative comments. This chapter covers how to stay patient, adjust your strategy when things aren't working, and handle criticism in a way that strengthens your business.

What to Do When You Don't See Results Right Away

One of the most common frustrations for small business owners new to social media marketing is not seeing results as quickly as they'd hoped. Maybe you've been posting regularly for a few weeks or even months, and the growth in followers or engagement just isn't where you expected it to be. It's important to remember that success on social media takes time, and it's completely normal not to see huge results right away.

Understanding That Social Media Growth Takes Time

Building a strong presence on social media doesn't happen overnight. It requires consistency, patience, and the willingness to learn as you go. You're not just looking to gain followers, but also to build relationships with your audience. These relationships take time to develop. Here's what to keep in mind:

- **Stay Consistent**: Even if you're not getting a lot of engagement right away, keep posting regularly. Over time, your efforts will start to pay off as you gain more visibility.
- **Engage with Your Audience**: It's not just about posting; it's about connecting. Make sure to respond to comments, ask questions in your posts, and show that you're interested in what your followers have to say.
- **Be Patient**: Social media isn't a magic bullet that will instantly bring in customers. It's a long-term investment in your brand's growth and reputation. Stick with it, and don't get

discouraged if you don't see results right away.

How to Tweak Your Strategy If You're Not Getting the Engagement You Expected

If you've been putting in the work and still aren't seeing the engagement you'd hoped for, it might be time to take a step back and evaluate your strategy. Here are some ways you can make adjustments:

- **Analyze Your Content.** Look at your posts that have performed well versus those that haven't. Are your followers more engaged with videos than images? Do certain topics get more comments or likes? Use these insights to guide your future content.

- **Adjust Your Posting Times**: When you post can be just as important as what you post. Experiment with different times of day to see when your audience is most active. Many social media platforms offer insights that show when your followers are online.
- **Try Different Formats**: If you've been relying on one type of content, like images, try mixing it up with videos, stories, or live streams. Different types of content perform better on different platforms.
- **Engage More Actively**: Don't just wait for your audience to come to you. Be proactive by commenting on other accounts, joining conversations in your niche, and using hashtags to reach new people.

Handling Negative Comments and Reviews

At some point, every business will face negative comments or reviews on social media. It's inevitable. However, how you handle these situations can make a big difference in how your brand is perceived. Responding with professionalism and turning a negative experience into a positive one can actually build trust with your audience.

Responding Professionally to Criticism

When you receive a negative comment or review, it's tempting to respond defensively, but it's important to stay calm and professional. Here's how to handle it:

- **Respond Quickly**: Ignoring negative feedback can make the situation worse. A prompt response shows that you care about your customers and are committed to resolving issues.

- **Be Polite and Empathetic**: Even if the criticism feels unfair, always respond with kindness and understanding. Acknowledge the customer's concerns, apologize for any inconvenience, and offer to help resolve the issue.

- **Take the Conversation Offline**: If the problem is complex, it's often best to move the conversation to private messages or email. This allows you to address the issue in detail without airing all the details publicly.

Turning a Negative Experience into a Positive Outcome

Negative comments don't have to be the end of the world. In fact, they can be an opportunity to show your professionalism and commitment to customer satisfaction. Here's how you can turn a negative experience into a positive one:

- **Fix the Problem**: If the customer's complaint is valid, take action to fix the issue. Whether it's a refund, a replacement product, or a personalized solution, showing that you're willing to make things right can turn an unhappy customer into a loyal one.
- **Show Transparency**: After resolving the issue, thank the customer for their feedback

and explain publicly (without too much detail) how you've addressed it. This not only helps rebuild trust with the person who left the comment but also shows others that you're a business that listens and cares.

- **Encourage Positive Reviews**: One way to counterbalance negative feedback is by encouraging satisfied customers to leave positive reviews. After a successful interaction or sale, kindly ask them to share their experience on social media or review platforms.

No business is immune to challenges on social media, but how you respond to those challenges is what really matters. By staying patient, tweaking your strategy when necessary, and handling negative comments professionally, you'll be better equipped to succeed in the long run. Remember, every hurdle is a chance to learn and improve. Stay focused, and don't let setbacks discourage you from building a strong social media presence for your small business.

CONCLUSION

Now that you've gone through this guide, you have a solid foundation to kickstart your social media marketing journey. Let's quickly recap the key steps to get you started:

- **Set Up Your Profiles**: Create professional profiles on the platforms that best suit your business. Make sure your bio, profile picture, and branding are consistent across all platforms.
- **Develop a Strategy**: Set clear goals, identify your target audience, and create a content calendar to plan and organize your posts.
- **Create Engaging Content**: Focus on content that resonates with your audience.

Experiment with images, videos, stories, and live streams to keep things fresh and engaging.

- **Grow Your Audience**: Engage with your followers, build relationships, and use organic methods like collaborations and influencer marketing to grow your reach.
- **Use Paid Ads**: Once you're comfortable, start experimenting with paid advertising to reach more potential customers and get more targeted results.
- **Manage Your Time**: Use social media management tools to save time, and consider outsourcing if managing your accounts becomes overwhelming.

- **Overcome Challenges**: Stay patient when results don't come immediately, and always respond professionally to negative feedback.

Social media is constantly changing, and what works today might not work tomorrow. That's why it's so important to keep learning, experimenting, and adapting your strategy. Don't be afraid to try new things and see what works best for your business. You don't have to be perfect right away—just keep moving forward, and you'll continue to grow and improve.

Next Steps for Your Social Media Success

Now that you have the basics down, what's next? Here are a few tips to keep you on the path to social media success:

- **Keep Learning**: Social media platforms are always evolving, so it's important to stay updated. Look for free online courses, blogs, and videos to continue learning about new trends and strategies.
- **Stay Updated with Trends**: Follow industry leaders, read social media news, and pay attention to what's working for other businesses in your niche. Being aware of trends will help you stay ahead of the curve and adjust your strategy as needed.

By following these steps and staying dedicated, your small business can thrive on social media. Keep experimenting, stay patient, and remember that success takes time. You've got everything you need to succeed—now it's time to put it into action!

www.ingramcontent.com/pod-product-compliance
Lightning Source LLC
Chambersburg PA
CBHW070424240526
45472CB00020B/1185